MY Love STORY!!

11

Story KAZUNE KAWAHARA

Art ARUKO

D1106732

MY love STORY!!

11

CONTENTS

STORY Thus Far...

Takeo Goda, a first-year high school student, is a hot-blooded guy who is 6'6" tall and weighs 265 pounds. Boys look up to him, but the girls he falls in love with all end up liking his handsome best friend, Makoto Sunakawa! But that all changes when Takeo saves Rinko Yamato from a groper on the train, and she becomes his girlfriend.

During summer break of their second year of high school, Yamato starts working at a cake shop. Ichinose, one of the pastry chefs there, tries to woo her! Takeo is disturbed by the appearance of this rival, but Yamato's love for Takeo is unwavering. Later, Takeo goes to Yamato's school festival. His presence wins him a special prize in the male beauty pageant!

Takeo has been feeling troubled lately because Yamato is so cute that he can't resist touching her. He tries to stay away from her, and Yamato becomes concerned that Takeo isn't acting his usual self. With Sunakawa's help, she learns Takeo's true feelings. And now, Takeo and Yamato are on separate school trips with nearly the same schedules!

Chapter 39 — 3

Chapter 40 — 49

Chapter 41 — 95

Chapter 42 — 139

MY
Love
STORY!!

MY love STORY!!

THE SKY SEEMS REALLY BIG HERE.
SO HOW HAVE THINGS BEEN WITH YOU AND YAMATO?
TH-THUMP
!!
SPLOOSH SPLOOSH
TAKEO! STOP!
ENOUGH WITH THE SPINNING!
SPIN SPIN
I HAVEN'T SEEN HER FOR A WHILE.
A WHOLE WEEK ALREADY...
I FEEL REALLY BAD ABOUT IT.
"I JUST NEED...
"...SOME TIME!"

WE'VE BEEN TEXTING THROUGH LINE.
SHE SOUNDS REALLY EXCITED.
EEEEE
Takeo! I'm so excited about our trip! Are you excited about yours?
I bought some new clothes and everything! When we're at the hotel, we don't have to wear our uniforms!
I haven't seen you for a while, so when I do, I might get overwhelmed with feelings!
Takeo! I love you!
...
SHE MUST BE FORCING HERSELF TO ACT THAT WAY.
...
THMP!!
TAKEO!
WE FINALLY HAVE FREE TIME TOMORROW!
I CAN'T WAIT!
WE'RE SO LUCKY THAT OUR ITINERARY OVERLAPS WITH THE GIRLS FROM KOIZUMI!
IT'S LIKE FATE OR SOMETHING!
Y-YEAH.

FREE TIME ...
OTARU'S A ROMANTIC HOT SPOT! IT'S A GREAT PLACE FOR COUPLES!
THMP
ARE YOU GOING TO SEE YAMATO TOMOR-ROW?
YEAH, THAT'S THE PLAN.
HMM...
GLEAM
I'M A LITTLE WORRIED.
YEAH, I CAN SEE WHY.
I MEANT I'M WORRIED ABOUT *YOU*.
YOU MISUNDER-STOOD.
BUT I CAN'T RUN AWAY FOREVER!

IT'LL BE FINE!
I WON'T MESS UP! SORRY FOR WORRYING YOU!
UH... OKAY.
WHAT IS IT?
NOTH-ING.
I WANT...
...TO TAKE GOOD CARE...
SPLSH
HA HA HA HA!
...OF YAMATO.
AHHH.

HEY, DO YOU HEAR THAT? GIRLS!
MAYBE IF WE SNEAK AROUND OUTSIDE WE CAN GET A PEEK INTO THEIR BATH!
C'MON, LET'S TRY IT!
BONK
OW!
LOOM
LOOM
WHAT WAS THAT FOR, TAKEO?
DON'T BE MAD. WHAT'S THE BIG DEAL?
I BET YOU'D LOVE TO SEE YAMATO—
OW!
AAAGH!
EEEK!
SPLOOSH
SPLASH
GAAH!
GAAH!

GAAH!
WHAT?! WHAT'S GOING ON?!
AAAGH!
TEACHER
BATH
GODA GOT MAD AT SOME GUYS WHO WERE GONNA GO SPY ON THE WOMEN'S BATH.
SPLASH
SPLASH
GAAH!
WHAT'S GOING ON?
WHY ARE THEY SITTING LIKE THAT?
GODA STOPPED SOME BOYS FROM SPYING ON OUR BATH.
GUESS THERE WAS A FIGHT.
OTHER PEOPLE HAVE TO USE THESE BATHS TOO!
COACH...!
GOT THAT?!
NOW GET BACK TO YOUR ROOMS.
RIGHT!
YES!
OKAY!

OSAMU...
...CAN'T KEEP HIS HANDS OFF ME.
THE SECOND WE'RE ALONE, HE STARTS!
EEEE!
WHAT THE HECK?
ARE YOU BRAGGING OR SOME-THING?!
EEEE!
EEEE!
EEEEE!
NO, I'M NOT!
WHEN HE DOES THAT, IT MAKES ME THINK HE ONLY WANTS ONE THING!
RINKO'S BOYFRIEND IS TOTALLY DIFFERENT.
HE TREATS HER WITH RESPECT!
OH...
GOTCHA.
OH...
RESPECT, HUH?

I'LL TAKE THE VERY BEST CARE OF YOU—!
ACTUALLY...
I'M SO JEAL-OUS!
AHH!
THAT'S TAKEO, ALL RIGHT!
BUT...
...HE DID SAY HE'D TAKE CARE OF ME...
...I'D REALLY LOVE IT IF I MADE HIM WANT...
...TO DO THAT STUFF.
I WOULDN'T MIND AT ALL IF HE—
...
HUH?!
WHAT?!
IF HE WHAT?!
RINKO!
YOU CAN'T DO THAT!
WE'RE IN THE MIDDLE OF A SCHOOL TRIP!

HEY, TAKEO!
THERE'S MORE TO LOVING SOMEONE THAN LOOKING OUT FOR THEM, RIGHT?
LOVE'S ABOUT GOING ON ADVENTURES TOGETHER TOO!
NO MATTER WHAT HAPPENS TO US, I WON'T BE AFRAID, NANAKO!
ZZZ...
IT'S TOO EARLY TO FALL ASLEEP!
I WAS SAYING SOMETHING PROFOUND!
I WOULDN'T SAY "PRO-FOUND."
COULD YOU QUIET DOWN?
AND YOU LOOK SCARY WHEN YOU'RE ASLEEP.
YAMATO...
I WON'T GIVE IN.
Takeo, we finally have free time tomorrow! I'm really looking forward to it! I can finally see you!
I PROMISED I'D TAKE CARE OF YOU FOR THE REST OF MY LIFE.

I MADE THAT PROMISE...
...IN MY HEART.
I WILL TAKE CARE OF YOU.
YOU CAN COUNT ON IT.

LINE UP!
ROLL CALL!
GROUP 7 IS HEADING OUT.
CURFEW IS 5 P.M.
OKAY!
ALL RIGHT! WE'RE HEADING TO THE WEST GATE AT SAPPORO STATION.
WE'LL MEET UP WITH NANAKO AND THE OTHERS THERE.
GOT IT.
札幌駅
SAPPORO STATION
THERE SURE ARE LOTS OF PEOPLE.
TWEET!
We're at the west gate!♫
TH-THMP

SHE'S HERE ?!
GLANCE
I HAVEN'T SEEN HER IN SO LONG THAT MY HEART'S POUNDING.
TMP
I FOUND YOU, TAKEO!
TH-THUMP

STAGGER
GASP!
NO! I CAN'T DO THIS! IF I LET MY GUARD DOWN, I'LL WANT TO TOUCH HER TOO BADLY!
FWIP
B-BMP, B-BMP
DAWW
HER HAIR'S EVEN SHINIER THAN USUAL!
WE'RE GOING TO DO OUR OWN THING!
SEE YOU LATER!
I'M MAKING HIS HEART RACE!
EEEEE!
...

OH
STARE
STARE
SUNA!
?!
SORRY, BUT...
...I NEED YOU TO STICK CLOSE FOR THE REST OF THE DAY.

SOMEHOW SEEING YOUR FACE CALMS ME DOWN.
PLEASE!
SURE, I DON'T MIND.
WHAT ARE YOU TALKING ABOUT?
GAH
SHE'S SO CLOSE!
I-IT'S NOTHING.
WANT TO GET GOING?!
TIME
9:44 OTARU
ARRIVING
KA-THUNK
KA-THUNK
SHE'S SO CLOSE!

...
ALL RIGHT, I'VE CALMED DOWN...
HUFF HUFF
BUT SO FAR WE'VE ONLY RIDDEN THE TRAIN!
AM I GONNA MAKE IT THROUGH THE REST OF THE DAY?!
OTARU STATION

I CAN SMELL THE OCEAN.
ALREADY? I CAN'T SMELL ANYTHING.
THAT'S AMAZING, TAKEO!
I DON'T HAVE TO WORRY ABOUT BEAR ATTACKS WITH YOU AROUND.
I DON'T THINK I CAN FIGHT A BEAR.
I DON'T THINK I'D BE ALLOWED TO FIGHT THEM.
YAMATO FEELS SAFE...
...BECAUSE SHE DOESN'T KNOW.
GRIN
I'M SORRY.
RIGHT NOW, I MIGHT BE EVEN MORE DANGEROUS THAN A BEAR.
OH, SHE KNOWS.

GLASS-BLOWING EXPERIENCE
I NEED...
HFF
I NEED TO FOCUS ON SOMETHING ELSE.
SHE'S SO CUTE ...!
HUFF
GASP!
...
...
SORRY.
IT'S OKAY.

PUFF
WOW!
THAT'S INCREDIBLE, TAKEO!
SHE'S SO CLOSE!
PUFF
I NEED...
...TO PULL MYSELF TO-GETHER.
WE HAVE TO LET YOUR WORK COOL DOWN.
WE'LL DELIVER THEM TO YOUR HOUSE. PLEASE WRITE YOUR ADDRESS HERE.
WOBBLE
WOBBLE
OKAY.
AAGH!
POINK
OH NO, THAT MUST HAVE BEEN UNPLEASANT FOR HER...

GRIN
YAMATO...
...SMILED.
SHE'S SO KIND...
I FILLED IN YOUR ADDRESS.
THANKS.

LOOK AT HOW MANY PEOPLE THERE ARE!
GRAB
!!
SO WE DON'T GET SEPARATED!
Y-YEAH ...
...
SQUEEZE

SQUEEZE♡
TH-THMP
SQUEEZE
!
TAKEO, YOU'RE GONNA BREAK MY ARM...
SORRY!
EEEE!
YAMATO SEEMS TO BE STICKING SO CLOSE TO ME TODAY!
OR MAYBE I'M BEING SELF-CONSCIOUS?
AND...
WAFT...

SHE SMELLS ...
...SO WONDERFUL...
GASP!
LEAN
NO! CALM DOWN!
SNIFF
SNIFF
SUNA SMELLS PRETTY GOOD TOO.
WHY? IS IT YOUR CONDITIONER?
DON'T YOU USUALLY SMELL SWEATY?
WHY WHAT?
I DON'T SWEAT THAT MUCH.
WOW!
LOOK HOW GORGEOUS THE CEILING IS!
SHE'S SO CLOSE!

I CAN FEEL HER BODY HEAT!
SUNA!
I NEED TO LOOK AT SUNA!
TURN
STARE
AH...
I'M CALMING DOWN...
THANKS, SUNA.
YOU SAVED ME.
IT'S SO PRETTY!
YAMATO KEEPS DOING THINGS WITHOUT MEANING TO.
...
YAMATO USUALLY DOES THINGS UNINTENTIONALLY...
...BUT I'M NOT SURE THAT'S WHAT'S GOING ON TODAY.

SHE REALLY DOES SEEM TO BE STICKING CLOSER THAN USUAL.
HOW DOES SHE USUALLY ACT?
...
SHE PROBABLY JUST FEELS SAFE BECAUSE SHE TRUSTS ME.
BUT EITHER WAY...
...YOU SAID YOU WOULDN'T KEEP RUNNING AWAY.
WOULDN'T YOU CALL THIS RUNNING AWAY?
YAMATO
(AT A DISTANCE)
YOU'RE... ...RIGHT...
...
YOU MIGHT BE MAKING THINGS AWKWARD BY TRYING TO SQUASH YOUR FEELINGS.

SOMETHING TERRIBLE MIGHT HAPPEN IF I DON'T!
REALLY?
BUT IT DOESN'T SEEM LIKE YOU'LL EVER BE CALM AROUND YAMATO.
YOU'LL HAVE TO TALK TO HER SOONER OR LATER.
YEAH...
YOU'RE ABSOLUTELY RIGHT.
OH! TAKEO!

DON'T YOU THINK THIS IS CUTE?
YEAH.
LISTEN...
AFTER THIS, WANT TO WALK AROUND TOGETHER?
SURE!
OKAY.
SUNA!
TAKE CARE OF THE OTHERS!
GET TO THE STATION BY 4:30, OR WE WON'T MAKE CURFEW.
GOT IT.
WHAT?! TAKEO'S GOING OFF ON HIS OWN TOO?!
I'M SO JEALOUS! UGH!
HA HA!

...
I KNOW I SAID I'D TALK TO HER...
...BUT I CAN'T TELL HER!

YESTERDAY...
YOU KNOW...
...I PUT A TREATMENT IN MY HAIR.
I LEFT IT IN AS LONG AS I COULD WHILE I WAS IN THE BATH.
IT'S SO GREAT THAT OUR SCHOOL TRIPS HAPPENED AT THE SAME TIME AND THAT WE CAN SPEND TIME TOGETHER!
YEAH, IT IS GREAT.

IT'S SO SMOOTH ...
AND MY NAILS...
SUCH SLENDER FINGERS ...
MY SCHOOL DRESS CODE DOESN'T LET US PAINT THEM.
SO I ONLY APPLIED A TOP COAT.
I TRIED MY BEST TO LOOK CUTE FOR YOU.
HEH!
I TOLD YOU EVERY-THING!

I LOVE HER!
YAMATO...

DON'T LET YOUR GUARD DOWN TOO MUCH!
I'M A TERRIBLE MAN...
I HAVE FEELINGS I CAN'T TELL YOU ABOUT...
THINGS YOU DON'T THINK ABOUT MUCH...
I CARE ABOUT HER SO MUCH... SHE MEANS MORE TO ME THAN ANYTHING IN THE WORLD.

...
UM...
ABOUT THAT.
TO BE HONEST...
...I ALREADY KNOW WHAT'S GOING ON IN YOUR HEAD.
WHAT IF I'VE BEEN STICKING SO CLOSE TO YOU ON PURPOSE?

WHAT...
...WOULD YOU DO?
WHEN I TOLD YOU...
...I WANTED TO HOLD HANDS...
I WANT TO HOLD HANDS WITH YOU!
...YOU'D SAID I COULD TELL YOU ANYTHING.
THROW IT ALL AT ME!
I CAN TAKE IT, NO MATTER WHAT!
AND SMILE!

IT GOES BOTH WAYS. YOU CAN THROW ANYTHING AT ME TOO.
AND...
...I'M SO HAPPY THAT BEING AROUND ME...
...MAKES YOU FEEL THE WAY IT DOES.

...
TH-THMP
TH-THMP
TWEET
Suna
It's time, Takeo.

OH!
GET TO THE STATION BY 4:30.
OH NO!
IT'S ALREADY AFTER 4:30!
Go on ahead.
We'll catch up.
CAN YOU RUN, YAMATO?
YES!
TMP
TMP
TMP
WHICH WAY IS IT?
BICYCLE
ARE WE GOING THE RIGHT WAY?

HUFF
HUFF
YAMATO!
!

"WHAT IF I'VE BEEN STICKING SO CLOSE TO YOU...
"...ON PURPOSE?
"WHAT WOULD YOU DO?"
WHAT DOES THAT MEAN?
WHAT DO YOU MEAN BY THAT, YAMATO?
OTAR STATION
OBEY TRAFFIC SIGNAL

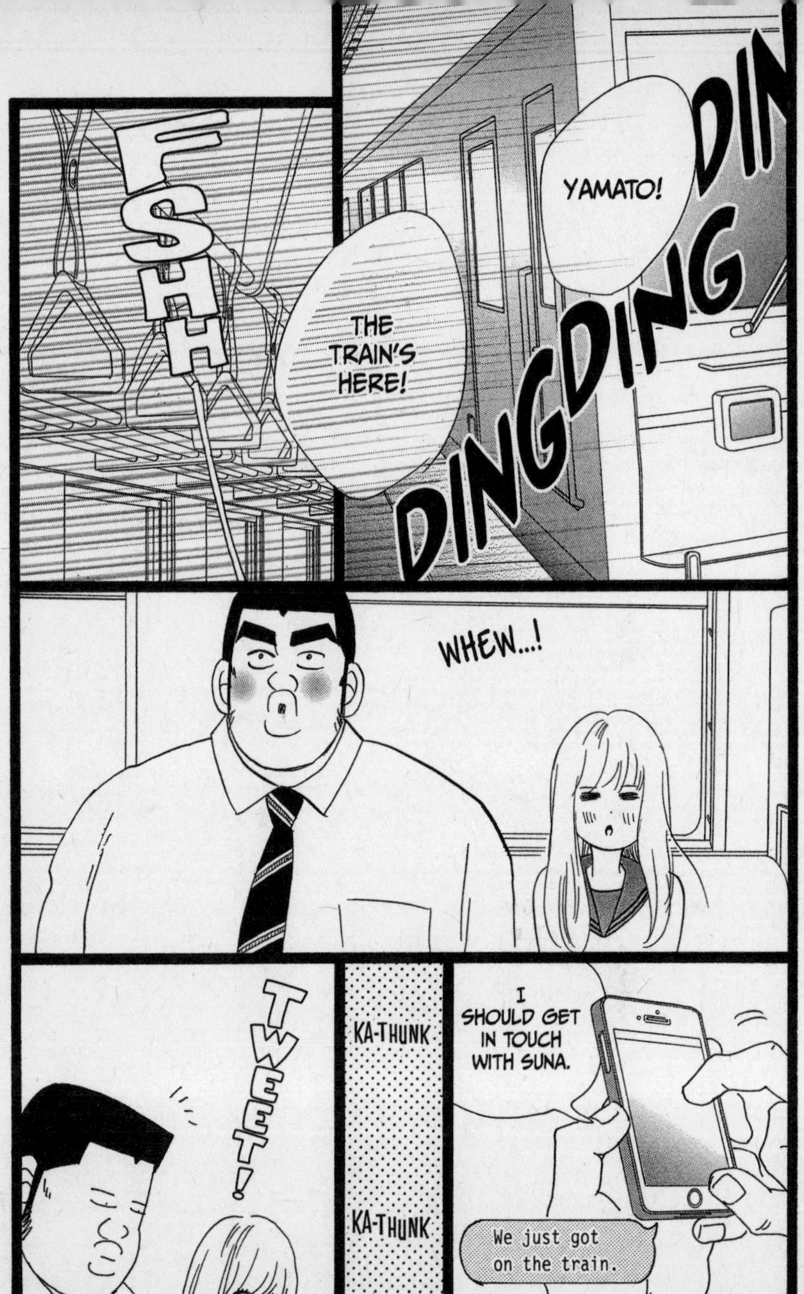

YAMATO!
DINGDINGDIN
THE TRAIN'S HERE!
FSHH
WHEW...!
I SHOULD GET IN TOUCH WITH SUNA.
We just got on the train.
KA-THUNK
KA-THUNK
TWEET!

I think you're probably on the wrong train, Takeo.
THIS TRAIN IS HEADED TO OSHAMANBE.
KA-THUNK
?!
THIS IS A ONE-MAN OPERATED TRAIN.
KA-THUNK
OH NO!!

"WHAT IF I'VE BEEN STICKING SO CLOSE TO YOU ON PURPOSE?
"WHAT WOULD YOU DO?"
...
KA-THUNK
KA-THUNK

SHIOYA STATION
HI, SUNA?
WE'RE NOT TOO FAR— AT A STATION IN SHIOYA.
BUT THE NEXT TRAIN WON'T BE HERE UNTIL 6:01.
WE'LL CATCH THAT TRAIN BACK.
OKAY, GOT IT.
ALL RIGHT.
SEE YOU LATER.
...

love STORY!!

MY love STORY!!

GLANCE
KRA—KL
SWIP

TH-THMP
TH-THMP
THERE'S...
しおや
塩谷
S 16
Shioya
おたる
Otaru
らんしま
Ranshima
...NO ONE ELSE AROUND.
TH-THMP
TH-THMP
"TO BE HONEST...
"...I ALREADY KNOW WHAT'S GOING ON IN YOUR HEAD.
"WHAT IF I'VE BEEN STICKING SO CLOSE TO YOU ON PURPOSE?
TH-THMP
TH-THMP

"WHAT WOULD YOU DO?"
WHAT DOES SHE MEAN BY THAT?
TH-THMP
TH-THMP
TH-THMP
TH-THMP
WHAT IS SHE TRYING TO SAY?
TH-THMP
...
LOOKS LIKE THERE ISN'T ANYONE HERE...
TH-THMP

"LOOKS LIKE THERE ISN'T ANYONE HERE..."
WHAT DOES SHE MEAN ...?
THERE'S NO ONE HERE.
WE'RE ALONE.
THERE'S NO ONE HERE.
IT'S JUST US TWO.
CALM DOWN !!
SHAKE SHAKE SHAKE SHAKE
SHE'S JUST SAYING THERE'S NO ONE HERE! THERE'S NO HIDDEN DEEP MEANING!
Y-YEAH!
THERE'S NO ONE HERE!

BEFORE CROSSING A RAILROAD, VALUE YOUR LIFE.
THERE'S NO DEEPER MEANING...
...RIGHT?!
...
IT'S CHILLY, HUH?
!
"IT'S CHILLY, HUH?"
WHAT DOES SHE MEAN?!
IT'S COLD.
I WANT TO WARM UP.
I WANT TO BE CLOSE TO YOU.
IT'S COLD.
I WANT TO BE CLOSE TO YOU.

CALM DOWN!
SHE'S JUST SAYING THAT IT'S COLD! THERE IS NO DEEPER MEANING!
GLANCE
YEAH!
IT'S KINDA COLD, HUH?!
STARE
THERE'S... NO DEEPER MEANING...
...RIGHT ?!
TAKEO...
I'M SORRY.

I...
...WAS SO HAPPY THAT BEING AROUND ME EXCITES YOU...
...THAT I WAS GETTING THAT CLOSE TO YOU ON PURPOSE.
KNOWING YOU FELT LIKE THAT WAS THRILLING.
EEEE!
I'M SORRY.
YOU'VE *ALWAYS* MADE MY HEART RACE.

YOU MAKE ME FEEL JUST AS WORKED UP...
...AS I MAKE YOU FEEL.
THAT DOESN'T MEAN IT'S THE SAME THING.
I'M A GUY, SO WHEN I GET WORKED UP, IT'S NOT SO SIMPLE.
HUH?
I THINK IT'S THE SAME.

I MEAN...
FOR A LONG TIME, I DIDN'T THINK I WAS ATTRACTIVE.
BUT NOW I KNOW I MAKE YOU FEEL THE WAY *YOU* MAKE *ME* FEEL.
...IT MADE ME SO HAPPY.
IS THAT WHAT YOU WERE THINKING?
YOU CAN DO ANYTHING YOU LIKE WITH ME.
I WON'T MIND, I PROMISE.

ARE YOU SURE IT'S ALL RIGHT ?!
STOP!!

THINK CAREFULLY BEFORE CROSSING A RAILROAD. VALUE YOUR LIFE.
STOP!! RAILROAD-CROSSING ACCIDENTS!
THINK CAREFULLY
BAM
VALUE
BAM
...

I'M GOING TO GET US...
...SOMETHING WARM TO DRINK!
DASH
SHH
KA-CHNK
I DON'T UNDERSTAND.
SHE SAYS IT'S ALL RIGHT...
...BUT I CAN'T TELL...
...WHAT'S OKAY AND WHAT ISN'T.
UGH!
I'M NOT CUT OUT FOR THINGS LIKE THIS.
SUNA...!

...
"WOULDN'T YOU CALL THIS RUNNING AWAY?"
"YOU'LL HAVE TO TALK TO HER SOONER OR LATER."
HE'S RIGHT.
IT'S NOT ABOUT IF I'M CUT OUT FOR THIS...
...OR IF I CAN DO IT.
I'M DATING YAMATO...
...SO I CAN'T SAY I DON'T KNOW WHAT TO DO.
I NEED TO THINK IT THROUGH ON MY OWN.
RIGHT, SUNA?!

EEEK!
GASP
OH NO!
I LEFT HER ALONE!
YAMATO!
DASH

WHAT'S WRONG? ARE YOU OKAY?!
A MOTH...
A MOTH?!
IT WAS HUGE...
IT SCARED ME.
YEAH, IT'S A BIG ONE.
IT'S OKAY NOW. IT FLEW OUTSIDE.
OH

KA-CHNK
KA-CHNK
TH-THMP
TH-THMP
TH-THMP

WE HAVEN'T HEARD FROM RINKO.
WHAT'RE WE GONNA DO? WE'RE REALLY CUTTING IT CLOSE.
札幌駅
SAPPORO STATION
WE'RE GONNA MISS CUR-FEW.
BUT WE CAN'T LEAVE HER BEHIND.
GO BACK AND EXPLAIN WHAT HAPPENED TO A TEACHER.
I'LL WAIT HERE IN CASE THEY CALL.
OH, OKAY.
THANKS.
WE'RE HEADING BACK TOO.
IT'D BE BAD IF OUR WHOLE GROUP WAS LATE.
LET US KNOW IF YOU HEAR FROM TAKEO.
SURE.

RINKO USUALLY SENDS US PICTURES.
I WONDER WHAT SHE'S DOING?
DO YOU THINK...
OH! MAYBE HER PHONE'S BATTERY DEAD!
YEAH! THAT'S GOT TO BE IT!
...

STATION

YAMATO...
I LOVE YOU.

THAT MAKES ME FEEL A LOT OF THINGS.
AND THAT MAKES ME WANT TO TAKE CARE OF YOU.
YEAH, I KNOW.

NO MATTER HOW YOU FEEL...
...I'LL NEVER FEEL LIKE YOU'RE NOT TAKING CARE OF ME.
LET'S WORK THIS OUT TOGETHER.
DON'T WORRY ABOUT IT BY YOUR-SELF.

I KNOW...
...I SAID I WAS FINE...
...BUT THERE ARE LOTS OF THINGS I DON'T KNOW MUCH ABOUT.
SO I MIGHT STILL BE SCARED.
I'LL LOOK AFTER YOU!
I WON'T EVER DO ANYTHING YOU DON'T LIKE.
HA HA
GOTCHA.

LET'S...
...DO THAT.
OKAY.
LET'S LOOK AFTER EACH OTHER, TAKEO.
SOUNDS GOOD.
THAT'S RIGHT...

YAMATO THINKS OF THINGS I NEVER WOULD.
I'M NOT THE ONLY ONE IN LOVE.
I SHOULDN'T ASSUME I'M DOING SOME-THING WRONG.
THERE ARE TWO OF US.
WE'RE IN THIS TOGETHER.
TAKEO...

YOU'VE HAD YOUR HANDS...
...ON MY FACE FOR A WHILE.
IT'S MAKING ME FEEL... YOU KNOW...
!!

THAT WAS NICE, WASN'T IT?
YEAH.
I WON'T RUN AWAY ANYMORE. IT'LL BE ALL RIGHT.
BECAUSE YAMATO ACCEPTS HOW I FEEL.

COME TO THINK OF IT...
...IF SHE WAS STAYING SO CLOSE TO ME TO GET ME WORKED UP...
GRAB
!!
POINK
AAGH!
SHE'S... A BIT OF A TEASE, HUH?
GAH
WHAT ARE YOU TALKING ABOUT?
SHE'S SO CLOSE!
THE 6:01 TRAIN TO SAPPORO IS TWO MINUTES BEHIND SCHEDULE.
INSTRUCTIONS FOR TRAVEL ON
OPERATED TRAIN
TH-THMP
!!
THERE'S SOMEONE ELSE HERE?!
THIS PLACE ISN'T EMPTY ?!
SHIOYA STATION

WE SHOULD GET IN TOUCH WITH EVERYONE.
RIGHT.
NANAKO AND THE OTHERS HAVE ALREADY HEADED BACK.
SAME WITH SUNA AND THE GUYS.
札幌駅
SAPPORO STATION
HUFF
WE'RE BARELY GONNA MAKE CURFEW!
HUFF
HUFF
DO WE TAKE THE SUBWAY TO YOUR HOTEL?
UH-HUH!
OKAY, LET'S RUN.
HUH? DON'T YOU HAVE TO GET BACK TOO?
I'M ALWAYS GETTING SCOLDED, SO IT'S NO BIG DEAL!
I'M TOO WORRIED TO LEAVE YOU ALONE! LET ME ESCORT YOU!
OKAY.

TMP
OH!
TMP
LOOK, THEY'RE WAITING FOR ME!
AAH... BUT I MIGHT NOT MAKE IT IN TIME...
TMP
THE ENTRANCE IS THIS WAY
YAMATO!
HUH ?

HOIST
DASH

IS RINKO BACK YET?
THIS IS BAD! ROLL CALL'S STARTING SOON...
WHAT SHOULD WE DO? WE HAVE TO GET BACK...
SWIP
AHH!
RINKO!!
I'M BACK.
WHERE DID YOU COME FROM?!
YOU SCARED ME!
WELL...
TAKEO...

LET'S GET GOING!
OKAY.
...
(REMEMBERING)
EEEEEE!!
?!
KA-THUNK
KA-THUNK
TWEET!

I made it back in time, Takeo!♥ Thank you!☆
I love you!♥
This trip was so much fun! I was so thrilled!♥♥
I SEE.
THAT'S GOOD.
I was even more thrilled.
No, me. >o<
No, me.
Me!
Me!
What are we doing?
This is so funny. ^▽^
I MADE IT TO THE STATION, BUT...

RRRING
RING
...HOW DO I GET BACK FROM HERE?
HELLO?
HEY, SUNA, IT'S ME.
HEY.
WHERE ARE YOU NOW?
UM... THE PLACE WHERE WE MET UP EARLIER TODAY.
SAPPORO STATION?
YEAH.
ALL RIGHT, I'LL HEAD OVER.

WEST TICKET GATE
WELCOME BACK.
THANKS.
WHY'D YOU COME DOWN?
I FIGURED YOU WOULDN'T REMEMBER THE WAY BACK.
THAT'S TRUE.
HOW'S YAMATO?
I DROPPED HER OFF AT HER HOTEL.
I SEE.
RELAX.
I HAVEN'T DONE ANYTHING YOU NEED TO WORRY ABOUT.
ACK!
IF I MISS CURFEW, I WON'T HAVE ANY FREE TIME AT NIGHT.
NO, WAIT. I ALREADY MISSED CURFEW.
I FILLED A TEACHER IN.

SORRY FOR MAKING YOU WORRY.
I WASN'T WORRIED, ACTUALLY.
EVERYTHING'S FINE NOW!
GOOD TO KNOW.
YOU SEEM PRETTY CONFIDENT.
I'M STILL...
...AWFULLY EXCITED, THOUGH.
...

AHHHH!!
WHAM
?!
THAT WAS CLOSE...
...
I'M HUNGRY.
WANT TO GET SOME RAMEN?
THERE'S FOOD AT THE HOTEL.
WHO'D GO FOR HOTEL FOOD OVER SAPPORO RAMEN?
THINK OF IT AS A SNACK.
AT 7 P.M.?

SAPPORO RAMEN
SAPPORO
SLURP
THIS IS KIND OF LIKE FREE TIME, ISN'T IT?
GUESS SO, YEAH.
HERE.
POINK
MUNCH
HERE.
POINK
BAMBOO SHOOTS

SET
TANTAN 700
SOBA 650
CANTONESE 600
BUTTER RAM 700
RAMEN 650
SHOYU RAMEN 600
580
THIS TRIP WAS PRETTY FUN.
YEAH.

MY
love
STORY!!

MY love STORY!!

MY PAN-CAKES ARE GONNA BURN!
HELP!!
...
DO YOU KNOW HOW TO MAKE THEM RIGHT?!
WELL, SURE.
BUT WHY ARE YOU MAKING PANCAKES?
KINDA OUT OF THE BLUE.
I FIGURED I'D MAKE SOME FOR MAKI.
MOM'S NOT HOME.
HMM...
IS THAT A CAST IRON PAN?
THAT'LL MAKE THINGS HARDER.
DO YOU HAVE A NONSTICK PAN?
HUH? YEAH.
YOU THINK SO?
THE HEAT'S TOO HIGH.
YOU'VE GOT IT ON THE HIGHEST SETTING.

YOU SHOULD START BY READING THE INSTRUCTIONS.
THEY'RE RIGHT ON THE BOX.
EASY HOKEMI
TOTTER
TOTTER
TOTTER
TRIP!!
TWIRL
SLAM!!
MAKI SURE IS AGILE, HUH?

ALL RIGHT!
SUCCESS!
IT'S A LITTLE BURNT THOUGH.
KINDA HUGE, NO?
IT'S GOT AN INTENSE FLAVOR.
SORRY.
YUB!
YUB!
WELL, I DO LIKE MY MEAT SLIGHTLY BURNT...
COOKING IS PRETTY TRICKY.
IT'S SOMETHING I HAVE TROUBLE DOING.
ISN'T IT HUGE?
AHM!
AHM!

I BET YAMATO WOULD MAKE AMAZING PANCAKES.
It's cold today!
There's snow, Takeo! The roads are all slippery.
The train's really late.
!
WOBBLE
SLIP
GRAB
FOCUS ON YOUR ENERGY CENTER WHEN YOU WALK.
TA... KE... O...!
"ENERGY CENTER" ?

TMP
TAKEO!
WAIT, YAMATO! DON'T RUN!
TMP
TMP
I'LL COME—
SLIP
!
GRAB

SLIDE
(FROZEN)
SLIDE
SLIDE
THUD
SPLASH
SHUP
S-SORRY, TAKEO ...
YOU FELL INTO A PUDDLE!
IT'S OKAY.
WHOOSH
KACHINK
(FRO-ZEN)
MY SKIN HURTS ...
THAT DOESN'T LOOK GOOD... WHAT IF YOU GET FROST-BITE?
MAYBE YOU SHOULD GO HOME FOR TODAY.
MAYBE...
THIS COULD BE BAD.

I'M SO SORRY, TAKEO!
DON'T WORRY ABOUT IT! I'LL TAKE A BATH AND THAW OUT.
KRRRNK
KRRRNK
WALK CAREFULLY ON YOUR WAY HOME!
OKAY...
KRRRNK
KRRRNK
...

SKRT
EEEEEE
...
I HOPE...
...YAMATO DIDN'T FALL.

MORNING! UGH, THE ROADS ARE ALL WET!
KOIZUMI GIRLS' ACADEMY
I KNOW, RIGHT?! THE SNOW MELTED SO FAST!
THE ROADS WERE SO SLIPPERY YESTERDAY! THE CARS WERE ALL HAVING TROUBLE.
I SLIPPED SO MUCH!
DID YOU FALL, RINKO?
NOPE. TAKEO SAVED ME.
RINKO'S BOYFRIEND IS THE BEST! TAKEO IS THE BEST!
...
BIIING
BOOONG
BIIING
THE TEACHER'S COMING. PUT YOUR PHONE AWAY.
...
HMM? WHY'RE YOU BOOKMARKING SO MANY SITES?

SERIOUS
R-RINKO?
TAKEO!
SHOEI HIGH SCH
LET'S ALL GO DO SOMETHING THIS WEEK! WANT TO?
I WANNA GO SKATING!
SURE.
LET ME CHECK WITH YAMATO.
(RESPONSE)
I'm pretty busy this week.
I'M SORRY!
THAT'S UNUSUAL.
Did something happen?
I'll tell you some other time!
It's
A
Secret!

A SECRET?
WHAT DID SHE SAY?
SHE'S BUSY THIS WEEK.
HUH? WITH WHAT?
SHE SAYS IT'S A SECRET.
WHAT?!
THIS IS BAD, TAKEO.
SHE'S OBVIOUSLY CHEATING ON YOU!
HUH?!
I LOVE YOU.
AND THAT MAKES ME WANT TO TAKE CARE OF YOU.

NO, SHE'S NOT.
THERE'S NO WAY.
SERIOUSLY? THAT'S SO BORING!
WHY AREN'T YOU PANICKING?
WHY WOULD I?
ARE YOU AT LEAST GONNA FOLLOW HER?
NOPE.
LET'S LOOK INTO IT!
NO.
BUT...
...I WONDER WHAT THE SECRET IS.
I AM KINDA CURIOUS.
WHAT COULD IT BE?
THE FACT THAT SHE TOLD YOU IT'S A SECRET PROBABLY MEANS SHE ISN'T REALLY TRYING TO HIDE IT.
SHE SAYS IT'S A SECRET...
...BUT THERE'S NO REASON TO FOLLOW HER OR INVESTIGATE.

闘拳
OPEN TO EVERYONE!
ACCEPTING STUDENTS
THANK YOU VERY MUCH!
I FOUND HER BY ACCIDENT! WHAT DO I DO NOW?
BOXING
RYONE!
DENTS

TMP
TMP
TMP
TMP
BOXING ...?
KARATE TRAINING HALL
↑ 2F
...

IS SHE SEEING HOW GOOD A FIGHTER SHE IS ?!
I WONDER WHAT SHE'S DOING...
I'M... SO... CURIOUS ...!
THANK YOU VERY MUCH!
OH!
OH!

TAKEO!
!
H-HEY.
I WASN'T FOLLOWING YOU OR ANYTHING. I SAW YOU BY ACCIDENT...
NO, NO, I KNOW THAT!
THIS IS THE ROUTE YOU TAKE TO SCHOOL.
AWW
BUT YOU ALREADY FIGURED IT OUT!
FIGURED WHAT OUT?! I HAVEN'T FIGURED OUT ANY-THING!
I...

I WANT TO BE STRONG!
LIKE YOU!
YOU ALWAYS SAVE ME WHEN I TRIP OR FALL OFF CLIFFS.
AND YOU GET ALL SCRAPED UP OR FROZEN!
BUT I DON'T MIND...
I KNOW.
BUT I MIND!

SO I WANT TO GET STRONG ENOUGH TO SUPPORT YOU.
I DON'T THINK THAT'S PHYSICALLY POSSIBLE.
I-I GUESS NOT.
BUT I WANT TO AT LEAST BE STRONG ENOUGH TO GET UP ON MY OWN WHEN I FALL.
...
DOES THAT MEAN YOU WANT TO KNOW HOW TO TUMBLE? HOW TO FALL SAFELY?
Y-YEAH!
THAT'S PROBABLY IT.

WANT ME TO TEACH YOU?
HUH?
I MIGHT BE ABLE TO TEACH YOU THE RIGHT WAY TO FALL.
WE COULD FIND SOMEWHERE TO PRACTICE.
OKAY!
I'LL LEARN FROM YOU!
DO YOU WANT ME TO GO EASY ON YOU OR PUSH HARD?
OH... UM...
PLEASE *DON'T* GO EASY ON ME!
OKAY!
...
I DIDN'T SEE THIS COMING...

MOM?
DO YOU HAVE MY TRAINING UNIFORM FROM WHEN I WAS LITTLE?
SURE. WHAT DO YOU NEED IT FOR?
I'M LENDING IT TO YAMATO.
THAT OLD THING?!
LET ME WASH IT FIRST.
I'LL BLEACH IT!
OKAY.
MUNICIPAL ATHLETIC
WHAT? THIS IS YOURS?
I USED IT IN GRADE SCHOOL. I FIGURED A TRACK SUIT WOULD PROBABLY BE TOO FLIMSY, SO YOU CAN USE THIS INSTEAD.
WOW! THANKS!
I'LL GET CHANGED!
OKAY.

DOES THIS LOOK OKAY?
I USED MY PHONE TO LOOK UP HOW TO WEAR IT PROPERLY.
I LOVE HER!!
THIS IS BAD.
SHAKE
SHAKE
SHAKE
YOU WERE PRETTY BIG EVEN IN GRADE SCHOOL, HUH?
ALL RIGHT.
READY TO BEGIN?!
WE'LL START WITH STRETCHES.
IF YOU DON'T STRETCH FIRST, YOU'LL HURT YOURSELF.
YEP!
GOT IT!

YOU'RE SO FLEXIBLE, TAKEO! THAT'S AMAZING!
I'M SO STIFF!
SHE REALLY IS.
MIND IF I GIVE YOU A PUSH?
OH, OKAY.
TH-THMP

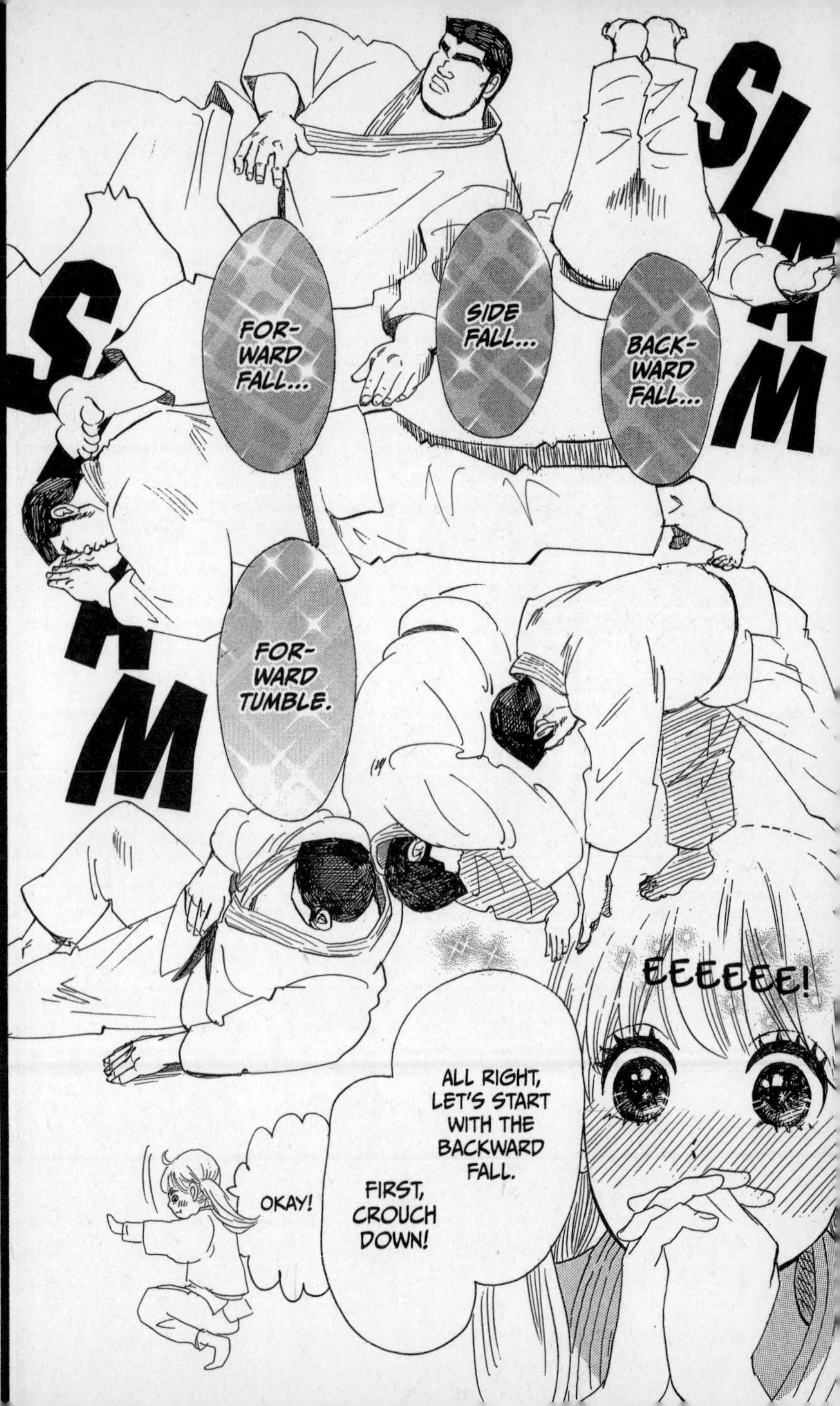
SLAM
FOR-WARD FALL...
SIDE FALL...
BACK-WARD FALL...
SLAM
FOR-WARD TUMBLE.
EEEEEE!
ALL RIGHT, LET'S START WITH THE BACKWARD FALL.
FIRST, CROUCH DOWN!
OKAY!

BONK
HOW DID THAT HAPPEN?!
?!
ARE YOU ALL RIGHT?
YEAH.
I SEE...
YAMATO ISN'T GOOD AT THIS.
I REALLY DON'T MIND GETTING WET OR GETTING HURT...
"BUT I WANT TO AT LEAST BE STRONG ENOUGH TO GET UP ON MY OWN WHEN I FALL."
...BUT...
...SHE SAYS THIS IS WHAT SHE WANTS TO DO.
ALL RIGHT, LET'S DO THIS.
START FROM A SITTING POSITION.
OKAY!

CURVE YOUR BODY!
TAKE IT SLOWLY!
STOP!
TWITCH
STOP!
TWITCH
!!
YOUR BELT! LOOK AT YOUR BELT!
DON'T LOWER YOUR EYES! USE YOUR WHOLE HEAD!
OH...

YES, SIR!
BELT!
SIR!
WE'RE NOT FINISHED YET!
YES, SIR!
THAT'S RIGHT.
THAT WAS GOOD.
YAAAY
NO! DO WHAT YOU DID BEFORE!
OKAY!
THAT'S RIGHT! LIKE THAT!
YES, SIR!
THAT GIRL IS AMAZ-ING...

HUFF!
HUFF!
HUFF!
ALL RIGHT, LET'S TAKE A BREAK.
YOU DID WELL.
SHA...
AHH!
WOW!
EEE!
RIGHT! BREAK TIME IS OVER!
SIR! ♥
WE'RE NOT DONE YET!
YES, SIR! ♥
TEN MORE TIMES!
YES! ♥

ALL RIGHT.
LET'S STOP THERE FOR TODAY.
CENTER
THANK YOU FOR EVERY-THING!
SURE!
FLAMES SUBSIDING...
HUFF
HUFF
HUFF
FIRE OUT...
WHEEZE
WHEEZE
WHEEZE
SHE LOOKS LIKE SHE'S GOING TO DIE!

I'M SORRY!
I PUSHED YOU TOO HARD!
HUH?
NO, I TOLD YOU NOT TO GO EASY ON ME.
I KNOW, BUT I SHOULDN'T HAVE TAKEN IT THIS FAR!
CAN YOU DRINK SOME WATER?
YES.
BUT DON'T FORCE YOURSELF TO DRINK!
OKAY.
I'M SORRY TOO.
FOR WHAT?
YOU'RE SO COOL WHEN YOU'RE TEACHING ME...
I GOT TOO GIDDY.

YOU'RE TRYING SO HARD TO TEACH ME AND I FEEL LIKE I SHOULD BE MORE SERIOUS, BUT...
I GET CARRIED AWAY...
SORRY!
OH...
W-WELL, SEEING YOU WEAR THAT TRAINING UNIFORM...
Y...
...
YOU'RE AWFULLY CUTE!
!!

BLUSH
WE'LL PRACTICE HARD!
OKAY!
DON'T CATCH A COLD!
ISTRY
TURN HERE
SHE MIGHT HAVE A LONG WAY TO GO...
...BUT I'M SURE SHE'LL LEARN.
SHE'LL BE FINE.
SLAM!
HEY, TAKEO.
MAKI KNOWS HOW TO TUMBLE...
SLAM!
TAKEO?
SLAM!
HEY, SHE'S ...

...
THINKING ABOUT TAKED.
EEEEE!
EEEEE!
ALL RIGHT, TIME TO PRACTICE!
WHACK
GAH!
!!

THE NEXT DAY...
COMPRESS
LAST NIGHT, I WAS PRACTICING MY MOVES...
AND MY HAND...
OH NO.
I DIDN'T TELL HER IT'S DANGEROUS TO PRACTICE ALONE.
PLIP PLIP PLIP

WHAT'S THE MATTER?!
I JUST... FEEL SO PATHETIC...!
IT'S BAD ENOUGH I CAN'T PROTECT YOU, BUT INJURING *MYSELF*?
PLIP PLIP
NO, IT'S MY FAULT FOR NOT TELLING YOU TO PRACTICE ON A CUSHION WHEN I'M NOT THERE TO SPOT YOU.
NO! IT'S NOT YOUR FAULT.
IT'LL BE FINE, YAMATO. I CAN WAIT!
WE'LL GET BACK TO IT AFTER YOU HEAL UP.
YEAH...

WHEN I WAS LITTLE...
...I USED TO TRIP A LOT.
I MEAN A LOT.
I SEE.
I WASN'T REMOTELY ATHLETIC, BUT I WAS FINE WITH THAT.
IT WASN'T A PROBLEM.
I WAS FINE WITH BEING A LITTLE SLOWER THAN EVERYONE ELSE.
BUT...
...AFTER I MET YOU...
...I WANTED TO GET STRONGER.

I'VE NEVER FELT LIKE THAT BEFORE.
WHEN SOME-ONE IS IMPORTANT TO YOU...
...THE STATUS QUO DOESN'T FEEL GOOD ENOUGH.
YOU WANT TO CHANGE...
...SO THAT YOU CAN TAKE CARE OF THEM.

YEAH...
I KNOW HOW THAT FEELS.
WHEN YOU FALL IN LOVE WITH SOMEONE...

I MADE PANCAKES THE OTHER DAY.
YOU DID?
THEY WERE BASICALLY CHARCOAL.
WHAT?
THEY SURE ARE TRICKY.
COULD YOU TEACH ME HOW TO MAKE THEM RIGHT SOMETIME?
SURE.
TAKEO! LOOK, THE HEAT IS TOO HIGH!
O-OH...

I'M READY TO LEARN!
FULLY RECOVERED
OKAY!
TURN YOUR HEAD TOWARD YOUR BELT!
YES, SIR!
NOW DO IT WHILE CROUCHING!
OKAY!
GOOD!
SLAM!
YEAH!
SLAM!
THAT'S IT, JUST LIKE THAT!
GLOW
ONE MORE TIME!
OKAY!

I FEEL LIKE I DID A LITTLE BETTER TODAY!
YEAH, GOOD JOB.
I WASN'T AS GOOD AS YOU THOUGH.
WELL...
I WASN'T SURE I COULD DO BETTER, BUT I DID!
YUP.
I WAS SURPRISED I COULD DO IT! IT WAS FUN!
YEAH!

SLAM
YAMATO CAN TUMBLE NOW...
I LOVE HER!
I DID IT!
ALL RIGHT!

MY love STORY!!

MY love STORY!!

POP
POP
?!
I'M SO HUNGRY...
THIS EARLY?
...
OH, THERE'S SUNAKAWA!
HE'S SO COOL!
HE AND GODA ARE ALWAYS TOGETHER.
I'M USED TO SEEING THEM TOGETHER NOW, BUT THEY'RE A STRANGE PAIR, HUH?
THEY'RE CHILD-HOOD FRIENDS, RIGHT?
YEAH, THEY'VE BEEN FRIENDS SINCE KINDER-GARTEN.

ONCE I ASKED MY EX-BOYFRIEND WHY THOSE TWO ARE SO CLOSE, AND HE GOT MAD AND TOLD ME I DIDN'T UNDERSTAND TAKEO.
MY BOY-FRIEND LIKES HIM TOO.
WHOA! WHAT'S THE DEAL WITH GODA?
HA HA HA!
OLD FRIENDS, HUH?
I SEE.
CHATTER
OH.
CHATTER
BYE BYE!
I'M MEETING UP WITH YAMATO. YOU COMING TOO?
NOT TODAY.
I'M STOPPING BY THE BOOK-STORE.
YEAH? WHAT'RE YOU GOING TO READ?
A TEXT-BOOK?
...
YOU'RE THINKING YOU SHOULDN'T HAVE ASKED, HUH?
SEE YOU!
YEAH.
SAY HI TO YAMATO FOR ME.
OKAY.

...
SWIP
HI, SUNAKAWA.
TAKEO!
HUH? WHERE'S SUNAKAWA TODAY?
HE WENT TO THE BOOK-STORE.
OH, GOT IT.
YAMATO, BEFORE I FORGET...
THE MARTIAL ARTS ROOM AT THE MUNICIPAL ATHLETICS CENTER IS GOING TO BE OPEN TO THE PUBLIC EVERY WEDNESDAY FROM NOW ON.
WANT TO KEEP UP YOUR TUMBLING THERE?
YEAH, I DO!

I BOUGHT A NOTE-BOOK.
I WAS THINKING OF USING IT AS A DIARY TO WRITE DOWN MY THOUGHTS OR WRITE ABOUT STUFF WE DO.
CHK CHK
WEDNESDAY
I PRACTICED JUMBLING WITH TAKEO.
CHK
CHK
CHK
CHK
...
EVERY-THING ABOUT HER...
...IS SO CUTE.
HA HA
IT DIDN'T STICK.
I LOVE HER.

HEY.
YOU DIDN'T GO TO THE BOOK-STORE?
HOW'D YOU KNOW?
YOU AREN'T CARRYING ONE OF THEIR BAGS.
OH...
YEAH...
OH!
GOOD EVENING, MAKOTO!
WELCOME BACK.
GOOD EVENING.

WHAT'S FOR DINNER TONIGHT, MOM?
I'LL CARRY THAT FOR YOU.
UNA! UNA!
WE'RE HAVING HOT POT.
SOUNDS NICE.
WANT TO JOIN US, MAKOTO?
YEAH, YOU SHOULD.
YOU'RE NOT DOING ANYTHING, ARE YOU?
I'LL TELL CHIAKI.
SUNA'S MOM
COME ON OVER.
EEEE! UNA! EEEE!
PLUP
BUP
MAKOTO, YOU'RE NOT EATING VERY MUCH.
I'M PROBABLY CHEWING TOO MUCH.
DON'T CHEW TOFU. SWALLOW IT.
DON'T JUST SWALLOW IT!
HERE'S SOME TEA, MAKOTO.
AND SOME TANGERINES.
THANK YOU SO MUCH.
THAT'S WHAT THEY CALL "MIDDLE SCHOOL SYNDROME," ISN'T IT?
TV
HUH? WHAT IS?
ISN'T THAT THE TERM FOR WHEN A YOUNG PERSON IS FRETTING OVER SOMETHING?
REALLY?

NICE TO SEE YOU, MAKOTO.
HEY!
GOOD EVENING.
WELCOME BACK.
WELCOME HOME.
HA HA HA!
HA HA!
THANKS FOR DINNER.
BYE.
YOU'RE WELCOME!
COME AGAIN SOON!
HEH
HMM? WHAT'S WITH THE SMILE?
JUST THINKING ABOUT HOW MUCH I LIKE YOUR FAMILY.
I SEE.
I LIKE YOUR FAMILY TOO.
WELCOME!
TROMP TROMP TROMP
I'M COMING IN!
GAH! I'M SORRY!
COVERED IN MUD
SUNA'S MOM
YOU'RE SO FULL OF ENERGY, TAKEO!
SUNA'S DAD
YOUR MOM'S SO ELEGANT, BUT SHE'S NICE AND EASY-GOING.
YOUR DAD TOO.
YEAH, THAT'S TRUE.

BAM
BUZZ...
BUZZ...
...
WE'RE HAVING HOT POT AGAIN TODAY.
OH? WHAT KIND ?
SUNA-KAWA!
YOU'VE GOT A VISITOR!

HMM?
WHO'S THAT?
I DON'T RECOGNIZE HIM.
FWP

WHO IS HE ?
HUH? SUNAKAWA'S TALKING TO THE TRANSFER STUDENT.
THE GUYS FROM CLASS 1 WERE SAYING A GOOD-LOOKING GUY TRANSFERRED IN.
OH ?
IS HE GOOD-LOOKING?
I'LL CARRY THAT FOR YOU.
WHERE ARE YOU HEADED?
HUH?
THANK YOU!
AWW♡♡
FWFF
TMP

I SEE. HE IS PRETTY GOOD-LOOKING.
HEY, THERE.
YOU DROPPED THIS.
YOUR HANDKERCHIEF.
HUH?
OH!
THANKS!
WHO SPILLED THIS WATER?! WIPE IT UP!
SIR!
I'LL CLEAN IT UP.
YOU'RE THE TRANSFER STUDENT, RIGHT?
YOU JUST GOT HERE. I CAN'T LET YOU CLEAN UP AFTER SOMEONE ELSE.
NO, I WANT TO.
I'D LIKE TO CONTRIBUTE TO MY SCHOOL. PLEASE LET ME DO IT.
HE'S GOOD-LOOKING AND SMOOTH!!
YEP, HE IS.

HMPH
SUNA?
DO YOU KNOW WHERE SUNA IS?
HE WENT OFF WITH THAT COOL GUY.
1-6
AGAIN?
THEY'RE SO GREAT!
WHEN TWO HOT GUYS ARE SIDE BY SIDE, IT MAKES THEM BOTH LOOK EVEN BETTER!
LOOKS LIKE THEY'RE HITTING IT OFF.
I LIKE WATCHING THEM!
...

HUH?
SUNAKAWA'S WITH THAT GUY AGAIN?
DO THEY KNOW EACH OTHER FROM SOMEPLACE ELSE?
NO, I DON'T THINK SO.
I KNOW EVERY-ONE SUNA KNOWS.
I GUESS I WOULDN'T KNOW ANYONE HE KNEW BEFORE MOVING HERE THOUGH.
HE WAS ABOUT THREE THEN.
HMM...
SO WHY'S HE ZEROING IN ON SUNAKAWA LIKE THAT?
I WONDER WHY TOO.
...
WHAT'S HAPPEN-ING?

SUNA AND I HAVE ALWAYS BEEN TO-GETHER.
WE GREW UP NEXT DOOR TO EACH OTHER AND WERE IN THE SAME CLASSES.
WE'RE ALWAYS TO-GETHER, AND...
...SUNA HAS NEVER REACHED OUT TO ANYONE.
THAT'S WHY THIS IS THE FIRST TIME I'VE SEEN HIM WITH SOMEONE I DON'T KNOW.
IT FEELS STRANGE.

ALL IT MEANS IS THAT SUNA...
...HAS HIS OWN LIFE!
WHAM!
OOOOOH!
GODA, THERE'S NOTHING ELSE I CAN TEACH YOU.
TEACHER
PFFT!
GO OFF TO THE SIDE AND DO YOUR OWN THING.
OKAY.
SHUP SHUP SHUP SHUP SHUP
HNGH! HNGH!
HNGH!
HE'S SUPER-HUMAN!
YOU'RE AMAZING, TAKEO!
HE NEVER RUNS OUT OF ENERGY!
HA HA HA!

I WANT TAKEO TO THROW ME! LET ME HAVE A GO, SIR!
NO WAY. IT'S TOO DANGER-OUS.
TERAMOTO'S ON THE JUDO TEAM. MAKE HIM FIGHT TAKEO!
OH.
I WANT TO SEE TAKEO DO JUDO!
YAMMER
IT'S NO BIG DEAL, SIR!
THERE'S THE TRANS-FER STUDENT.
YAMMER
COME ON, TAKEO! DO IT!
YAMMER
YAMMER
HIS CLASS IS JOINING OURS.
FOR GYM.
FWP
I SEE...
YEAH!
HE REALLY IS GOOD-LOOKING.
SWIP

HOOOO
SLAM
THAT'S SO COOL!
TAKEO!
YOU'RE INCREDIBLE AS ALWAYS.
NAH, I STILL HAVE ROOM FOR IMPROVE-MENT.
HOW'S YAMATO DOING WITH THIS?
SHE'S GOTTEN PRETTY GOOD!
WANT TO GIVE IT A TRY? KNOWING HOW TO FALL CORRECTLY IS HANDY.
HA HA!
I'LL PASS, THANKS.
...

SUNAKAWA!
SOME-ONE'S HERE FOR YOU!
...
THAT'S TRUE, IT DOES.
THAT GUY...
I DON'T MIND THAT HE LIKES SUNAKAWA, BUT...
...IT FEELS LIKE HE'S TAKING HIM AWAY FROM US.

BIIING
BOOONG
CHATTER
CHATTER
HEY, SUNA, WANT TO WALK HOME TOGETHER?
OH...
ACTUALLY, UH...
I'M WALKING WITH TANAKA, THE NEW GUY IN CLASS 1.
OH, RIGHT.
THE GUY WHO KEEPS STOPPING BY.
OH, YOU KNOW HIM?
YEAH.
HE ASKED ME.
I SEE.
I UNDERSTAND.

HUH?
WHERE'S SUNAKAWA?
HE HAD PLANS WITH SOMEONE ELSE.
OH...
I FEEL LIKE I HAVEN'T SEEN HIM IN A WHILE.
I MADE SNOW-BALLS TODAY.
SAME HERE.
I HAVEN'T WALKED HOME WITH HIM IN TEN DAYS OR SO.
BUT WE STILL WALK TO SCHOOL TOGETHER.
HE'S MADE FRIENDS WITH A TRANSFER STUDENT.
MUNCH MUNCH
WHAT? REALLY?
THAT'S RIGHT.
THIS IS THE FIRST TIME...
...I'VE GONE SO LONG WALKING HOME WITHOUT HIM, EXCEPT DURING SUMMER BREAK.

WHAT'S THE TRANSFER STUDENT LIKE?
A HANDSOME GUY.
OH, REALLY?
WELL, I THINK *YOU'RE* THE HANDSOMEST!
O-OH.
THANKS...
YAMATO...
THAT'S KINDA RANDOM.

I WONDER IF SUNA WILL WALK HOME WITH THAT GUY TOMORROW.
KNOCK KNOCK!
KA-CHAK
!!
WHAT'S THE MATTER?
NOTHING.
JUST A SECOND!
RUSH RUSH
FWISK FWISK
WHAT'S GOING ON?
NOTHING REALLY.
JUMP

...
FWSH
FWUMP
ARE YOU OKAY?
NEED A SHOULDER MASSAGE?
NO, THANKS.
I LIKE MY BONES INTACT.

WHAT'S GOING ON?
TAKEO, YOU'RE REALLY CLOSE.
OH, SORRY.
SHUP
ACTUALLY, I'M SLEEPY. I'M GONNA HEAD HOME.
OKAY.
CHAK
WHAT WAS THAT ALL ABOUT?

I WANT TO GO ON A DATE HERE SOMETIME.
IT LOOKS SO GREAT.
SUNA'S NOT HERE.
HE'S WITH THAT GUY AGAIN.
WHAT'S THE SITUATION WITH YOU GUYS AND THE GIRLS?
WE'RE LIKE DATING IN A GROUP.
OR SOMETHING.
SUNAKAWA, DOES THAT INCLUDE YOU?
WAIT, WHERE'D HE GO?
THAT NEW KID AGAIN?
IT'S RARE FOR A GUY TO STOP BY FOR SUNAKAWA.
IS IT?
AS RARE AS A GIRL COMING TO SEE YOU.
I SEE.
IT'S HARD TO INTERRUPT TWO HOT GUYS.

IT WOULD'VE BEEN HARD TO EVER TALK TO SUNAKAWA IF HE HADN'T BEEN WITH YOU.
REALLY?
CUZ HE'S SO QUIET! AND WHEN HE'S ALONE, HE'S ALWAYS READING. YOU NEVER KNOW WHAT HE'S THINKING.
A MAN OF MYSTERY?
THAT'S PART OF HIS CHARM, HUH?
HA HA HA!
BUT WHEN I SAW YOU TWO TOGETHER, I REALIZED WHAT KIND OF PERSON HE WAS.
HE'S PRETTY EASY TO TALK TO AFTER THE FIRST TIME.
HE HAS GOOD STUFF TO SAY.
HE'S A GREAT GUY.
YEAH.
THAT'S RIGHT.
HE IS A GREAT GUY.
THAT'S PROBABLY WHY THAT TRANSFER STUDENT WANTS TO BE FRIENDS WITH HIM.

BIIING
SOME PEOPLE CAN JUST TELL.
BOOONG
BIIING
HEY, SUNA, WANT TO WALK HOME?
OH, UM...
TANAKA NEEDS SOME STUFF FOR SCHOOL AND WANTED ME TO GO SHOPPING WITH HIM.
OH?
WILL IT BE OKAY WITH JUST THE TWO OF YOU?
WON'T YOU HAVE A LOT TO CARRY?
I CAN COME TOO—
NO, THAT'S OKAY.

SHOCKED
I'LL GO BY MYSELF.
IT'LL BE FINE.
OKAY...
SURE...
I GUESS ...
YOU'VE GOTTEN A LOT BETTER.
REALLY? HOORAY!
...
MUNICIPAL ATHLETIC CENTER

WHAT'S THE MATTER?
HMM?
IT'S NOTHING.
STARE
STARE
IT'S JUST...
...SUNA HAS A NEW FRIEND.

IT'S SOMEONE I DON'T KNOW.
THAT'S NEVER HAPPENED BEFORE.
IT FEELS STRANGE.
THAT'S ALL.
TAKEO...!
YOU'RE SUNAKAWA'S BEST FRIEND!

N-NO.
IT'S NOT LIKE THAT!
HEH HEH...
IT'S NOT LIKE THAT, YAMATO!
I MEAN...
MAYBE... THAT'S TRUE?
I'M ALWAYS...
...RIGHT THERE WITH HIM.

I STARTED THINKING THAT...
...WITHOUT REALLY REALIZING IT.
"YOU'RE SUNAKAWA'S BEST FRIEND!"

TAKEO!
YAMATO!
OH, YUKIKA...
HI! IT'S BEEN A WHILE.
YES, IT HAS!
BOW
TAKEO, YOU HAVE TO DO SOME-THING!
HMM?
IT'S THAT NEW STUDENT—THE REALLY GOOD-LOOKING GUY.
THE ONE WHO KEEPS HANGING AROUND SUNAKAWA!

HE'S NASTY AND TWO-FACED!
HE'S WHAT?!
THANKS FOR TODAY.
NO PROB-LEM.

LOOK AT THOSE TWO COOL GUYS!
ABOUT YOUR FRIEND...
THAT BIG GUY, I MEAN. YOU TWO DON'T HAVE MUCH IN COMMON, HUH?
HE PROBABLY DOESN'T UNDER-STAND YOU.
HEY, I WAS WONDERING...
DO YOU NOT HAVE A GIRLFRIEND BECAUSE YOU WANT TO FOOL AROUND WITH A BUNCH OF GIRLS?
IT'S NOTHING LIKE THAT.
THEN WHY'RE YOU SINGLE?
WAITING FOR SOME PERFECT LOVE?
DO YOU THINK YOU'LL FIND SOMEONE WHO'LL UNDERSTAND EVERYTHING ABOUT YOU?

THAT'LL NEVER HAPPEN!
CONNECTIONS BETWEEN PEOPLE ARE TOTALLY FAKE.
I'VE CHANGED SCHOOLS MORE THAN TEN TIMES.
THAT'S HOW I KNOW.
ONCE YOU'RE OUT OF SIGHT, YOUR "FRIENDS" STOP CONTACTING YOU.

STICK WITH ME.
YOU'LL DO BETTER WITH ME THAN HIM. YOU'LL SEE.
YOU SHOULD CHOOSE YOUR FRIENDS MORE CAREFULLY.
HE ALWAYS SAYS AWFUL THINGS.
IT SEEMS LIKE...
...HE'S JUST USING HIS FRIENDS.

USING THEM ?
USING HIS FRIENDS ?
DOES THAT MEAN HE'S USING SUNA ?
IS THAT TRUE ?!
VRR
VRR
Incoming Call Takeo

VRR
HELLO?
SUNA! WHERE ARE YOU RIGHT NOW?!
HAVING COFFEE AT THE BOOK CAFÉ BY THE STATION.
IS THAT NEW GUY WITH YOU?
UM...
YEAH.
ALL RIGHT, GOT IT.
I'M ON MY WAY OVER. STAY PUT!
DOOO

DOOT... DOOT... DOOT...
...
?
ZOOM
TO BE CONTINUED...

VOLUME 11! THANK YOU SO MUCH!!

I WAS GIVEN THE SHOGAKUKAN MANGA AWARD! THANK YOU!
I RECEIVED THE KODANSHA MANGA AWARD A WHILE BACK...
BUT THAT WAS THREE YEARS AGO! I'M SO THRILLED!!

I'VE BEEN KNITTING LATELY... JUST ACRYLIC SCRUBBING PADS THOUGH.

I REALIZED SHE THOUGHT IT WAS LIKE CREDIT CARD FRAUD OR COUNTERFEITING.

Hello! Thank you very much for picking up volume 11! In 2015, I went to so many places: Sendai, Okinawa, Osaka, Tokyo and an empty station (in Hokkaido). Traveling is amazing! It was all for work, but I'm hoping to go to those places again. I had so much fun... I think I really enjoy taking trips! I like moving to new places too. I'd like to visit the cities and towns where you all live. I love imagining places I've never been to as I walk! Anyway, I hope to see you again in Volume 12!

2016
KAZUNE KAWAHARA

Thank you for picking up volume 11! Sometimes, when I'm asked to sign copies of My *Love Story!!*, I'll draw knockoffs of Yamato and Takeo. It's a strange feeling... Aruko's art is definitely the best, isn't it? I've gotten used to drawing knockoffs of Takeo and his friends though.

– Kazune Kawahara

ARUKO is from Ishikawa Prefecture in Japan and was born on July 26 (a Leo!). She made her manga debut with *Ame Nochi Hare* (Clear After the Rain). Her other works include *Yasuko to Kenji*, and her hobbies include laughing and getting lost.

KAZUNE KAWAHARA is from Hokkaido Prefecture in Japan and was born on March 11 (a Pisces!). She made her manga debut at age 18 with *Kare no Ichiban Sukina Hito* (His Most Favorite Person). Her best-selling shojo manga series *High School Debut* is available in North America from VIZ Media. Her hobby is interior redecorating.

This time, I tried to make the cover look like a retro storybook. The year 2016 has begun. Recently, I've had the sudden desire to make curry! I'd like to get better at making it. And I think I'll try a more athletic weight-loss plan. I'd also like to create manga with spirit! I hope I'll see you around again.

– Aruko

MY LOVE STORY!!

Volume 11
Shojo Beat Edition

Story by **KAZUNE KAWAHARA**
Art by **ARUKO**

English Adaptation ♡ **Ysabet Reinhardt MacFarlane**
Translation ♡ **JN Productions**
Touch-up Art & Lettering ♡ **Mark McMurray**
Design ♡ **Fawn Lau**
Editor ♡ **Amy Yu**

ORE MONOGATARI!!
© 2011 by Kazune Kawahara, Aruko
All rights reserved.
First published in Japan in 2011 by SHUEISHA Inc., Tokyo.
English translation rights arranged by SHUEISHA Inc.

The stories, characters and incidents mentioned in this publication are entirely fictional.

No portion of this book may be reproduced or transmitted in any form or by any means without written permission from the copyright holders.

Printed in the U.S.A.

Published by VIZ Media, LLC
P.O. Box 77010
San Francisco, CA 94107

10 9 8 7 6 5 4 3 2 1
First printing, February 2017

www.viz.com

RATED T FOR TEEN
PARENTAL ADVISORY
MY LOVE STORY!! is rated T for Teen and is recommended for ages 13 and up. This volume contains suggestive themes.
ratings.viz.com

www.shojobeat.com

Can love trump a cursed life?

Sawako's a shy, lonely, pure-hearted student who just happens to look like the scary girl in a famous horror movie! But when she manages to befriend the most popular boy in school, will her frightful reputation scare off her best chance for love?

kimi ni todoke
From Me to You

By Karuho Shiina

Find out in the *Kimi ni Todoke* manga—
BUY YOURS TODAY!

Winner of the 2008 Kodansha Manga Award (shojo category)

On sale at **www.shojobeat.com**
Also available at your local bookstore or comic store.

Shojo Beat MANGA from the HEART

RATED T FOR TEEN ratings.viz.com

VIZ media www.viz.com

KIMI NI TODOKE © 2005 Karuho Shiina/SHUEISHA Inc.

Is this girl a devil in disguise...
or a misunderstood angel?

A Devil and Her Love Song

Story and Art by Miyoshi Tomori

Meet Maria Kawai—she's gorgeous and whip-smart, a girl who seems to have it all. But when she unleashes her sharp tongue, it's no wonder some consider her to be the very devil! Maria's difficult ways even get her kicked out of an elite school, but this particular fall may actually turn out to be her saving grace...

Only **$9.99 US / $12.99 CAN** each!

Vol. 1 ISBN: 978-1-4215-4164-8
Vol. 2 ISBN: 978-1-4215-4165-5
Vol. 3 ISBN: 978-1-4215-4166-2
Vol. 4 ISBN: 978-1-4215-4167-9

Check your local manga retailer for availability!

RATED T FOR TEEN ratings.viz.com
Shojo Beat
VIZ media
www.viz.com

AKUMA TO LOVE SONG © 2006 by Miyoshi Tomori/SHUEISHA Inc.

Don't look for the
FULL MOON
lest demons find you.
SAKURA HIME
The Legend of Princess Sakura
Story and Art by
Arina Tanemura
Creator of Full Moon
and Gentlemen's Alliance †
ISBN: 978-1-4215-3882-2
$9.99 USA | $12.99 CAN
Available Now
at your local bookstore and comic store
Shojo Beat
RATED T TEEN
ratings.viz.com
VIZ media
www.viz.com
SAKURA-HIME KADEN © 2008 by Arina Tanemura/SHUEISHA Inc.

A Collection of Shorts by One of Shojo's Biggest Names

A one-volume manga featuring early short stories from the creator of *Full Moon*, *The Gentlemen's Alliance †*, *I•O•N* and *Time Stranger Kyoko*.

Find out what makes Arina Tanemura a fan favorite—buy *Short-Tempered Melancholic and Other Stories* today!

Shojo Beat MANGA from the HEART

On sale at www.shojobeat.com

Also available at your local bookstore and comic store.

KANSHAKUDAMA NO YUUTSU © 1996 by Arina Tanemura/SHUEISHA Inc.

RATED T FOR TEEN ratings.viz.com

VIZ MEDIA www.viz.com

honey and clover
By Chica Umino
An eccentric group of students band together to face life's uncertainties. Set in a Tokyo art college, *Honey and Clover* blends comedy and pathos to bring to life a very unique set of individuals.
Shojo Beat Manga
honey and clover
Read the *Honey and Clover* manga series—available now!
Shojo Beat
On sale at:
www.shojobeat.com
Also available at your local bookstore and comic store.
HONEY AND CLOVER © 2000 by Chica Umino/SHUEISHA Inc.
RATED T+ FOR OLDER TEEN
ratings.viz.com
VIZ media
www.viz.com

You may be reading the **wrong way!!**

IT'S TRUE: In keeping with the original Japanese comic format, this book reads from right to left—so action, sound effects, and word balloons are completely reversed. This preserves the orientation of the original artwork—plus, it's fun! Check out the diagram shown here to get the hang of things, and then turn to the other side of the book to get started!

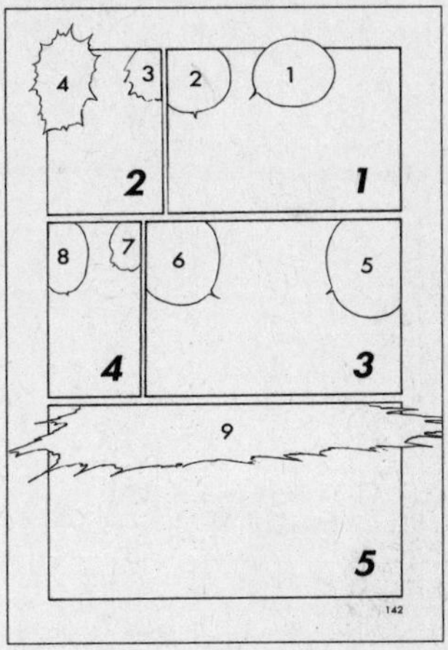

But can she tell who the real villain is?

The Earl & the Fairy

Story & Art by Ayuko
Original Concept by Mizue Tani

Lydia Carlton is a fairy doctor, one of the few people with the ability to see the magical creatures who share our world. During one of her rare trips to London to visit her father, Lydia's quiet life is suddenly transformed when she is rescued from kidnappers by a mysterious young man!

Only **$9.99** each!
($12.99 in Canada)

Vol. 1 ~ ISBN: 978-1-4215-4168-6
Vol. 2 ~ ISBN: 978-1-4215-4169-3
Vol. 3 ~ ISBN: 978-1-4215-4170-9
Vol. 4 ~ ISBN: 978-1-4215-4171-6

Check your local manga retailer for availability!

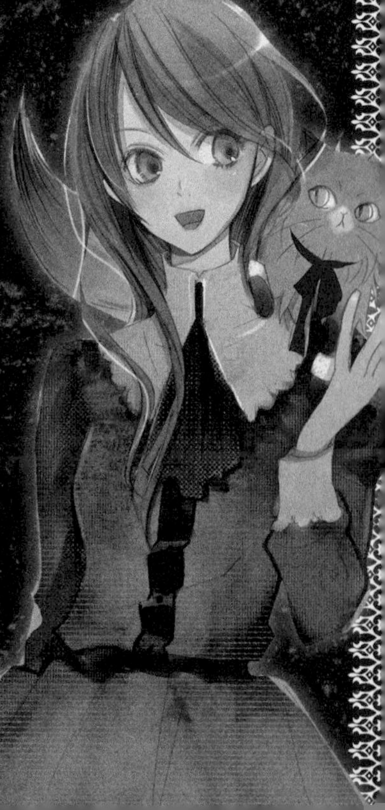

viz media
www.viz.com
Shojo Beat
RATED T FOR TEEN ratings.viz.com

HAKUSHAKU TO YOSEI-COMIC EDITION-
© 2008 by Mizue Tani, Ayuko/SHUEISHA Inc.